Beautiful

AUSTRALIA

Fannie Bay, Darwin, is the site where Keith and Ross Smith landed their aircraft in 1919, completing the first flight from the UK to Australia. (Higgins)

First Edition 1987
Published by Child & Associates Publishing Pty Ltd
5 Skyline Place, Frenchs Forest, NSW, Australia, 2086
Telephone (02) 975 1700; facsimile (02) 975 1711
Reprinted 1987
Second Edition 1989
Reprinted 1990
First published 1982 by Golden Press Pty Ltd, Sydney

©Text: Child & Associates Publishing Pty Ltd 1982, 1987, 1989
©Photographs: Bill Andrews, Trevern Dawes, Neil Hermes,
    Geoff Higgins, Peter Solness, Ian Wigney 1982, 1987, 1989

Designed and typeset in Australia
Typeset by Keens, Sydney
Printed in Singapore by Kyodo-Shing Loong
Printing Industries Pte Ltd

Material used in this book previously appeared in *Presenting Australia.*

National Library of Australia Cataloguing-in-Publication Data

Beautiful Australia.

   2nd ed.
   Includes index.
   ISBN 0 86777 254 9.

   1. Australia—Description and travel—1976–   —Views.

994.06'3'0222

Beautiful
AUSTRALIA

CHILD & ASSOCIATES
AN ALL-AUSTRALIAN PUBLISHER

Contents

The Balconies, the Grampians. Wind and water have eroded many of the sandstone rock formations of these stark ranges into bizarre shapes. (Higgins)

Overleaf: The Cazneaux Tree at Wilpena — a favourite haunt of photographers. Harold Cazneaux, famous photographer of the Australian pictorial movement, first photographed this tree in 1937, calling it 'The Spirit of Endurance'. (Dawes)

Introduction: Australia's Early Days

Australia, the world's largest island and smallest continent, has a rich diversity of scenery and landform from arid red heartland, cropping land and pastures, to snow-capped mountains.

The Aborigines took possession of this land aeons before the white man came. They have left a rich heritage in their folklore, and their rock and tree [...]. They were the first to draw the unique fauna such as the kangaroo, the koala, and the platypus.

Although the Dutch recorded sighting Australia in 1606, it was Captain James Cook, sailing from England in the *Endeavour*, who finally put Australia on the world's maps in 1770. Methodically, he charted the east coast, and went ashore near Cape York to hoist the Union Jack and formally possess the land in the name of King George III.

Australia's recorded history only covers about two hundred years, yet it is rich and colourful. Colonizing began when Britain needed somewhere to send criminals from her overflowing gaols. The arrival of the First Fleet in 1788, under Captain Arthur Phillip, makes exciting reading. He discovered a perfect natural harbour and named the site of his camp Sydney, after the Home Secretary, Lord Sydney.

Slowly, sheep farming developed, and the wool trade became the mainstay of the colony in its early years. Then in 1851 gold was discovered near Bathurst. Gold fever was on, and people poured in from all over the world. Many stayed, and gave the growing colony a boost in population and in demand for goods and services.

In 1802 Britain took formal possession of Tasmania, and shipped many of the more dangerous criminals from New South Wales there. Historic Port Arthur, near the capital city of Hobart, has many reminders of convict days.

By 1821 New South Wales settlers were objecting to the influx of convicts and the present site of Brisbane, in Queensland, was opened up. When the rich potential of the pasture lands of the Darling Downs was realized the free settlers soon followed.

For a while the large land mass in the west of the continent remained undeveloped. Then, in 1826, Governor Darling sent an expedition of marines and convicts to form a settlement. The convict period in Western Australia was only a brief eighteen years but many of the lovely old bridges, public buildings and roads are its legacy. The beautiful city of Perth now stands on the north bank of the Swan River, a site originally described as 'the most healthy area of the Globe. . .'

When gold was discovered it triggered a rush to Western Australia. Kalgoorlie became known as the Golden Mile, the richest gold area the world had ever known.

South Australia really opened up from within when, in 1820, Charles Sturt made his great journey down the Murray River to its source, and spoke enthusiastically of fertile plains and scenic ranges. The present site of Adelaide owes its spaciousness to the foresight of Colonel William Light, then Surveyor-General. It was his wise planning which provided for the lovely parklands surrounding the city.

Further exploration of the interior by John McDouall Stuart, who succeeded in crossing the continent from Adelaide to the Indian Ocean, revealed the potential of large tracts of good grazing land to the north. South Australia received permission to annex the Northern Territory, which it administered for many years. In 1911 the Commonwealth Government formally took over the Northern Territory, and self-government was granted in 1978.

The Port Phillip district, near what is now Melbourne, in Victoria, began with a little colony of Englishmen. 'Squatters' soon settled in the area, and were legally granted land in 1836. A land boom began and within five years the fertile soil was being farmed. The city of Melbourne owes its layout of wide streets to the foresight of one of the surveyors, Robert Hoddle.

The individual states were eventually united to form a Federal Commonwealth. In 1901, Federation became a fact, and Edmund Barton became Australia's first Prime Minister. Melbourne was the temporary capital until 1927, when the federal government moved to the newly-formed Australian Capital Territory. Canberra's city plan was the brainchild of architect Walter Burley Griffin, and its system of roads and careful placing of public buildings afford pleasant vistas from most parts of the city.

Each of the States reflect, in the distinctive architecture of their old buildings, much of their historic beginnings, and there is now genuine concern to preserve this national heritage.

Australia today is a bustling, highly developed nation with migrants from thirty different countries. As well as primary produce from farming there are vast mineral resources, and many secondary industries.

The States have developed rapidly during the two colourful centuries of their history. Between them they reveal the diversity of climate and scenery, and the fascinating variety of flora and fauna, which comprise Australia.

Above: Parrots at the Currumbin Bird Sanctuary on the Gold Coast. Founded in 1947, the Sanctuary is now part of the National Trust. (Queensland Tourist & Travel Corporation)

Below: Fraser Island, the largest island off Queensland's coast and the largest sand island in the world, is a unique area of freshwater lakes, tangled rainforest, swamp and heath vegetation and endless beaches. (Solness)

Queensland and Northern Territory

Brisbane, Australia's third largest city where convict buildings are shaded by modern sky scrapers. (Solness)

Right: The Big Pineapple at the Sunshine plantation, 115 kilometres from Brisbane. The 16 metre high replica of a pineapple contains educational displays and observation deck. The adjacent building contains a Polynesian style restaurant and tropical market. (Queensland Tourist & Travel Corporation)

Right: Parasailing at Southport on the Gold Coast. (Higgins)

Facing page: A quiet corner of solitude at Gladstone Harbour, Queensland's largest tonnage port. (Higgins)

Top: Cook's Pillar, Cooktown.
Captain Cook beached here in
1770 to repair damage after
running aground on the
Barrier Reef. (Solness)

Above: The dingo, Australia's
only species of wild dog, was
probably brought into the
country by the Aborigines.
(Dawes)

Right: Pandanus line the
banks along a peaceful
stretch of the Katherine River.
(Higgins)

The pelican is found throughout Australia wherever suitable areas of water exist. (Higgins)

Castle Hill towers over the Sacred Heart Cathedral in Townsville, the major city of north Queensland. (Higgins)

A rich silver-lead deposit was discovered at Mt Isa by John Campbell Miles in 1923. He named the area after his sister, Isabella. Today Mt Isa Mines operate one of the largest silver-lead mines in the world. Copper and zinc are also mined and processed here. (Solness)

The residence of the Northern Territory Administrator, Darwin. Built in 1870, this is one of the few buildings that has withstood the ravages of World War II bombing and Cyclone Tracy. The Northern Territory obtained self-government in 1978 and became, in effect, Australia's seventh state. (Higgins)

Sculptures by William Ricketts at 'Pitchi Richi' museum, Alice Springs, depict the Dreamtime of the Aboriginal people. (Higgins)

Facing page: Lake Eacham, a crater lake 730 metres above sea level in the Atherton Tableland. (Solness)

Stockmen at the Laura rodeo.
This small township of less than
150 people is 2168 kilometres
north-west of Brisbane. (Higgins)

Above right and right: East
Alligator River Crossing — the
entrance to the
eight million hectare Arnhem
Land Aboriginal Reserve.
(Higgins, Dawes)

Facing page: Millstream Falls —
at 65 metres wide, they are the
widest falls in Australia.
(Solness)

Facing page: One of the major attractions of the Northern Territory is the Katherine Gorge National Park where the river flows between towering, brilliantly coloured walls. Aboriginal rock paintings form huge murals high above the flood level on the gorge walls. (Higgins)

Right: Aboriginal children, Arnhem Land. (Higgins)

Below: Katatjuta — the Olgas — literally 'place of many heads', is a spectacular group of massive rock domes rising steeply from the level desert in the 'Red Centre' of Australia.
The 30 domes are separated by narrow vertical chasms and the highest point is 450 metres above the spinifex plain. (Higgins)

18

Facing page: Charred and smoking remains of a bush fire in the Gulf country. (Solness)

Above: The Devil's Marbles — a cluster of gigantic boulders piled up on each other. Aboriginal legend is that the boulders are eggs laid by the mythical Rainbow Snake. (Solness)

Ayers Rock, the world's largest monolith, rises 348 metres above the plain and is 9 kilometres in circumference. The sheer immensity of this great rock and the unusual colouring, which changes from orange to purple at sunrise and sunset, has made it one of the natural wonders of the world. A sacred dreaming place of the Aboriginal people, the base of the rock is undercut with caves in which the Aboriginals have left galleries of rock paintings in charcoal and ochre. (Dawes, Higgins)

Facing page, above:
Sydney's most distinctive
landmarks: the soaring
sails of the Opera House
and the splendid arch of
the Harbour Bridge.
(Higgins)

Restored and in operation
in The Rocks district, this
postbox is a relic of the
Victorian era. (Higgins)

New South Wales

Sydney's Opera House —
the city's centre of the
performing arts — beside
the harbour on Bennelong
Point.

Facing page, below left:
Beaches are the village green
of Sydney's summer social
life. Manly is a favourite surf
beach on the northern side of
the city. (Higgins)

Facing page, below right:
Chinese gardens at the
entertainment development
at Darling Harbour, Sydney.
(Higgins)

Above: Doyles on the Beach restaurant at Watsons Bay, Sydney. (Higgins)

Below: Sheer cliffs of the Kanangra Walls in the Blue Mountains. On a clear day one can see Sydney's Harbour Bridge — more than 100 kilometres away — from this vantage point. (Higgins)

Left: Autumn at the town of Mt Wilson in the Blue Mountains. (Higgins)

Above: The Breadknife — a gargantuan, 90-metre-high sliver of rock in the Warrumbungle Ranges. (Higgins)

Right: Massed colour at the Tulip Festival held every October in Bowral. (Green)

Formerly a bustling gold mining town with a population of 30 000 and 52 hotels, the now sleepy Hill End has been proclaimed a national historic village. The Royal Hotel is the only hotel still standing. (Higgins)

Below: The start of the Bridge to Bridge Race along the Hawkesbury. Here seen at Dangar Island. (Higgins)

Facing page, below right: Bridge over the Murray near Hume Weir — a man-made inland lake ideal for water sports. (Solness)

Facing page, above: Warrumbungle National Park contains some of the most spectacular scenery in Australia. Aboriginal for 'broken mountains', the Warrumbungle Ranges comprise deep gorges and precipitous rock faces — a mountaineer's paradise. (Higgins)

Facing page, below left: Established in 1894, Ku-ring-gai Chase National Park is the home of a wide range of birdlife, including the cheeky kookaburra. (Dawes)

Right: Jacaranda trees lining the wide streets of Grafton. A glorious Jacaranda Festival is held annually in November. (Wigney)

Below: Trial Bay Gaol near Kempsey. The building, with walls 5.5 m high and 45 cm thick, took its first complement of prisoners in 1886. The gaol was closed in 1903, although it was used again during World War I to confine German internees. (Higgins)

Bottom: Some of the hand-crafted toys at Sugar Creek Toymakers, a great tourist attraction at Smiths Lake.

Facing page: Rich dairylands border the Bellinger River on the north coast of New South Wales. (Andrews)

Stockton Bridge,
Newcastle. (Higgins)

Parkes, first settled in
1862 when gold was
discovered, is now the
commercial and
industrial centre for the
surrounding agricultural
area. (Wigney)

Golden Gully, Hill End. The huge Beyers and Holtermann nugget was found in this area in 1872. (Higgins)

Above: The Myall River at the delightful town of Tea Gardens, near Port Stephens. (Higgins)

Below left: Newcastle Mall. (Higgins)

Below right: Catamarans at Belmont, one of the main resorts on the beautiful Lake Macquarie. (Higgins)

Above: Lake Jindabyne, Snowy Mountains. (Wigney)

Facing page: Downhill skiers, Kosciusko National Park. (Higgins)

Above: Fitzroy Falls tumble through rainforest in Morton National Park. (Higgins)

Below: New Parliament House on Capital Hill, Canberra, was opened by HRH Queen Elizabeth II in our Bicentennial year. (Hermes)

The lush, beautifully landscaped Royal Botanic Gardens provide a peaceful retreat for Melbourne city dwellers. (Higgins)

The shady green banks of the Yarra are a delightful place to relax. (Andrews)

Victoria and Tasmania

Melbourne city, capital of Victoria, overlooks the
Yarra River. Founded in 1835 by John Batman
and John Pascoe Fawkner, Melbourne has an
unruffled style and elegance. (Higgins)

Sovereign Hill, a major reconstruction of a gold-mining settlement just outside the centre of Ballarat. (Wigney)

Loch Ard Gorge, Port Campbell National Park, was the scene of a dramatic shipwreck over 100 years ago — only two men survived. (Dawes)

Facing page: The Murray River at Echuca. Situated at the junction of the Murray, Campaspe and Goulburn Rivers, Echuca was once Australia's largest inland port. (Wigney)

Mildura, on the Murray River, was once a busy port with more than 100 vessels passing through in a six-month season. The lock system of the Murray was completed in 1928 and today Mildura is still Australia's paddle steamer capital with restored vessels gracefully plying the river to serve the tourist trade. (Higgins)

Floral clock at Ballarat's Botanical Gardens. (Higgins)

This page: Winter months bring snow to Mt Buffalo and skiers flock to the area for downhill and crosscountry skiing. In the summer, cascading waterfalls and interesting rock formations are the scenic attractions. Hume and Hovell named the mountain 'Buffalo' as its humped granite mass, rising to almost 1800 metres, reminded them of a bison. (Higgins)

Lakes Entrance — home port for a very large fishing fleet — lies at the eastern end of the Gippsland Lakes which form the largest inland network of Waterways in Australia. (Dawes)

Left: Once a bustling seaport serving the rich mineral fields of Tasmania's west coast, today Strahan's main industry is tourism. (Tasmanian Department of Tourism)

Below: Church at Port Arthur — a penal settlement from 1830 to 1877. Port Arthur is the only substantial convict ruin in Australia and has been preserved as a scenic reserve. (Tasmanian Department of Tourism)

Left: Tasmania's main pastoral district is the picturesque Midland area between Oatlands and Perth. It is noted for its high quality merino wool and stock raising. (Solness)

Above: The Derwent River near New Norfolk. (Tasmanian Department of Tourism)

Left: The vehicular ferry returns to Kettering from Bruny Island, historic landing spot of Captain Cook in 1777. (Tasmanian Department of Tourism)

Russell Falls in the Mt Field National Park. (Andrews)

Facing page: Mt Wellington towers 1270 metres over Hobart, capital of Tasmania. (Tasmanian Department of Tourism)

Above: The baroque fountain was brought to Launceston from Paris in 1859. (Tasmanian Department of Tourism)

Right: Wrest Point Casino, Hobart — the South Pacific's centre of glamour and sophistication. (Tasmanian Department of Tourism)

Below: Ross Bridge, a monument to artistic convict craftsmanship. The three symmetrical arches all bear intricate contemporary patterns of colonial days. (Tasmanian Department of Tourism)

Cradle Mountain at the northern end of the
Cradle Mountain— Lake St Clair National Park.
(Tasmanian Department of Tourism)

A colourful display at the Royal Botanic
Gardens set in the Queen's Domain, Hobart.
(Andrews)

Above: Fern study at the Mt Field National Park — home of a variety of mosses, ferns, lichens and fungi. (Solness)

Water is carried through huge pipelines to the Tarraleah power station below. Most of Tasmania's electricity is generated by water power. (Tasmanian Department of Tourism)

Facing page: Spacious and well planned, the city of Adelaide is situated on the Torrens River between the Gulf of St Vincent and the Mount Lofty Ranges. During the 1880s Adelaide was variously described as 'City of Churches', 'Farinaceous Village' and 'Model City'. (Higgins)

Right: 'The banks of the channel, with the trees and the rocks, were reflected in the tranquil waters whose surface was unruffled save by the thousands of wild fowl that rose before us…' wrote Charles Sturt about the Murray in 1830. (Solness)

Below: Chateau Yaldara winery at Lyndoch in the Barossa Valley. (Dawes)

South Australia and Western Australia

Above: Admiralty Arch, on Cape du Couedic, Kangaroo Island. Pounding seas have slowly eroded the limestone to produce this spectacular formation. (Dawes)

Below: Opal is the reason for the tiny township of Coober Pedy in the heart of the South Australian outback. Opals were discovered here in 1911 and today there are hundreds of mines. (Higgins)

Right: 'Old man with Arms Crossed' — a baobab tree on the outskirts of Derby. Having great ability to store water in their trunks these trees are native to the drought prone northern areas of Australia. (Dawes)

Above: Underground church, Coober Pedy. 'White fellow's hole in the ground' is the Aboriginal name for Coober Pedy. It is an appropriate name as temperatures reaching 54°C have persuaded most of the population to live underground for protection against the harsh climatic conditions. The underground buildings stay at a constant temperature of 24°C all year round. (Higgins)

Right: Vibrant cliff formations of Red Bluff, Kalbarri, form a striking contrast to the blue of the Indian Ocean. (Higgins)

Above: Morialta Falls. (Solness)

Right above: Marla bore — symbol of that precious commodity of the South Australian outback — water. (Solness)

Right: London Court, an Elizabethan-style arcade running from Hay Street Mall to St George's Terrace. (Western Australian Tourism Commission)

Facing page: Perth, capital city of Western Australia, lies on the fertile north banks of the Swan River. Named and established by Captain James Stirling in 1829, it is now the fifth largest city in Australia. (Higgins)

Facing page: A Waugul monolith depicting Cook's voyage, Yanchep. (Dawes)

Right: The fish are running at Kalbarri, Western Australia. (Andrews)

Below left: Mudflats and mangrove-lined drainage channels stretch out from Five Rivers Lookout at Wyndham, the most northerly port in Western Australia, servicing the Kimberley beef industry. (Higgins)

Below right: Folded bands of coloured rock enclose this circular pool, Hamersley Range. (Higgins)

Fortescue Falls in the Hamersley Range. (Higgins)

Above: Naturally sculpted out of granite, Wave
Rock, in Hyden, is estimated to be 2700 million
years old. This remarkable 15 metre high
formation is streaked with water stains
varying in colour from deep grey and ochres to
reds and a pale sandy tint. (Higgins)

Below: Rugged, coloured hills surrounding
Kununurra — the only town established in the
Kimberleys this century. (Dawes)

Left: The high cliffs of Brachina Gorge to the north of Wilpena in the Flinders. (Higgins)

Below left: Built in 1888, the Broome Court House was originally used as a Cable House to hold transmitting equipment for the underwater cable linking to Java. (Higgins)

Below right: In the 1900s Broome was a bustling pearling centre with 400 luggers plying the coast in search of the precious gem. Today the heyday is over, but some luggers still fish for young pearl oysters. (Higgins)

Facing page: Geikie Gorge near Fitzroy Crossing, one of the most colourful and spectacular accessible river gorges in north-west Australia. Large permanent waterholes in this area are the home of sharks, saw-fish and freshwater crocodiles. The distinctive change of colour on the rock face marks the high water mark in the wet season. (Higgins)

Facing page: Waterlillies at Dawn Creek in the West Kimberley. (Dawes)

Right: Windjana Gorge, soaring 90 metres above the riverbed, is one of the most striking features of the Napier Range. (Dawes)

Below: Bold, rocky headlands of the coast near Esperance thrust out into the turbulent Southern Ocean. (Higgins)